W9-BCT-409

COOL

CRAYONS, CHALKS & PAINTS

CRAFTING CREATIVE TOYS & AMAZING GAMES

REBECCA FELIX

Checkerboard Library

An Imprint of Abdo Publishing
abdopublishing.com

ABDOPUBLISHING.COM

Published by Abdo Publishing, a division of ABDO, PO Box 398166, Minneapolis, Minnesota 55439. Copyright © 2016 by Abdo Consulting Group, Inc. International copyrights reserved in all countries. No part of this book may be reproduced in any form without written permission from the publisher. Checkerboard Library™ is a trademark and logo of Abdo Publishing.

Printed in the United States of America, North Mankato, Minnesota

102015
012016

Content Developer: Nancy Tuminelly
Design and Production: Mighty Media, Inc.
Editor: Paige Polinksy
Photo Credits: Julie Clopper/Shutterstock, Mighty Media, Inc., Shutterstock

The following manufacturers/names appearing in this book are trademarks:
Crayola®, Elmer's®, Gedney®, KitchenAid®, Slice of the Moon™

Library of Congress Cataloging-in-Publication Data
Felix, Rebecca, 1984- author.
  Cool crayons, chalks & paints : crafting creative toys & amazing games / by Rebecca Felix.
     pages cm. -- (Cool toys & games)
  Includes index. 2286
  ISBN 978-1-68078-048-2
1. Handicraft--Juvenile literature. 2. Crayons--Juvenile literature. 3. Paint--Juvenile
literature. I. Title. II. Title: Cool crayons, chalks and paints.
  TT160.F455 2016
  745.59--dc23
                          2015033041

CONTENTS

ART SUPPLIES

Do you like creating art? What art supplies do you use? You've likely used paints, markers, crayons, colored pencils, and chalks before. But have you ever made any of these art supplies? That is what artists did for thousands of years!

Creating art is one of the world's oldest **pastimes**. To make art, ancient people first had to create their own supplies. They dug up clay from the earth. They ground **pigments** from plants and minerals and mixed them with water to create ink and paint. Paint was also made using eggs, oils, and even **saliva**!

Today, paints, crayons, and chalks of all kinds can be bought in stores around the world. Some are very **advanced**. Chalks are glittered and scented. Crayons come in more than 100 colors. And some paint even glows in the dark!

LIGHT AT NIGHT

Glow-in-the dark paints are made with a pigment called phosphor. This pigment collects and stores light energy. The energy is visible when the paint glows in dim or dark settings!

MAKING COOL, COLORFUL ART SUPPLIES

Think of art supplies you've used. Crayons come in little paper jackets, sharpened and ready to use. Paints are premixed and sealed in airtight containers. And pens and markers hold **pigments** in polished tubes.

Many people around the world are hard at work each day to create these and other art supplies. Workers haul lumber on large trucks. They use machines to saw and shape wood into sleek colored-pencil tubes. In other factories, workers mix paint pigments and **mediums** in huge vats using industrial machinery.

PERMANENT COLOR

Pigment colors are permanent. They do not **dissolve** in water. These colors are used in paints, crayons, and colored pencils. Dye colors do dissolve in water. They can be washed out. Markers and pens use dyed ink.

Crayon makers blend liquid wax with pigments and pour the mixture into molds. These art supplies are wrapped, boxed, and sent to the store. They inspire artists of all ages to create works of art!

BECOME A TOY MAKER

THINK LIKE A TOY MAKER

Today's art supplies come in plenty of colors, **mediums**, and vessels. They can be bought in all types of stores. But you can also make many at home!

As you work on the projects in this book, think about what mediums you want to work with. Consider what supplies you want to make. Look at the photos. Do they inspire you to create different features? Maybe you want to make paint in wacky colors. Or add glitter to a crayon recipe. Go for it! Search at home or in craft stores for fun things to add to your creations.

HAVE FUN!

Finished toys are meant to be fun to play with. And creating them should be too! Don't worry if something doesn't turn out quite how you wanted. Just try again or work with what you have made. Get creative! Then have fun using your handmade supplies to create original works of art.

PIGMENT, PASTE, PAINT!

Today, machines make huge amounts of paint all at once. But manufacturers use the same basic process art-supply makers have used forever. First, **pigments** are ground up. Then all ingredients are mixed into a paste. This can take hours, or even days! Some manufacturers then let the paint age for several more days or weeks. Finally, the paint is packaged and ready to use.

MATERIALS

blackberries

cutting board

dish soap

foam brushes

glow-in-the-dark powder

measuring cups

mesh strainer

mixing bowl

old crayons

oven mitt

paint stir stick

paintbrush

paper plate

scissors

silicone
ice cube tray

small trinkets

string

tempera paint

waxed paper

white all-purpose
glue

white vinegar

SAFETY SYMBOLS

Some projects in this book use sharp objects or hot tools. This means these projects need adult help. You may see one or more safety symbols at the beginning of a project. Here is what they mean:

 HOT

 SHARP

MEGA-LAYER CRAYON

CREATE A COLOSSAL CRAYON WITH SEVERAL LAYERS OF COLOR!

PREPPING THE CRAYONS

1 Unwrap the paper from all crayons. Break the crayons into small pieces.

2 Line the bowls with waxed paper. Separate the crayon pieces into bowls by color. Then trim any extra paper, so the paper lies just over the lip of the bowl.

(continued on next page)

MATERIALS

old crayons
waxed paper
microwave-safe
  bowls
scissors
silicone ice cube tray
oven mitts
string
paint stir stick

ceramic plate

SPECIAL NOTE
This project has several fast, short steps stretched over many hours.

CREATING THE BASE LAYER

1 Fill one cup of the ice cube tray with broken crayons. This will be the innermost layer of your crayon.

2 Have an adult help you heat the oven to 250 degrees Fahrenheit (120°C). Cook the crayons for 10 minutes or until melted.

3 Wearing oven mitts, remove the tray from the oven. Set it on a countertop. Cut an 8-inch (20 cm) piece of string. Carefully place the end of one string in the center of the melted wax.

4 Let the crayon cool for 10 minutes. Then place the tray in the freezer for 10 minutes.

RE-DIPPING THE CRAYON

1 Lay a sheet of waxed paper on top of the plate.

2 Remove the tray from the refrigerator. Carefully pop the crayon from the tray. Set it and the plate aside.

3 Decide the color of your next layer. Put the bowl with this color in the oven. Bake at 250 degrees Fahrenheit (120°C) for 10 minutes or until melted.

4 Wearing oven mitts, remove the bowl from the oven. Have a helper pick up the hardened crayon and dip it into the bowl. Twist and turn the bowl until the crayon is covered with the melted color. Or, use a stir stick to flip the crayon a couple times.

(continued on next page)

5 Remove the crayon and set it on the plate. Set the plate in the refrigerator for 15 minutes.

6 Remove the crayon from the refrigerator. Repeat steps 3 through 5 with the other bowls of crayon pieces. The hardened crayon will grow larger and larger, creating layers of color!

7 Once the crayon has as many layers as you like, trim the string. Then reveal the colors by creating artwork!

SMOOTH MOVES!

Don't worry if your crayon looks lumpy. Its surface will smooth out as you color with it!

CRAYON KINGS

Crayola crayons are the most widely known brand of crayons. And their history goes back more than 100 years!

In 1885, cousins Edwin Binney and C. Harold Smith started a company selling **pigments**. Then they began experimenting with other supplies. In 1903, they mixed wax with pigments. The mixture hardened into a colorful writing utensil. The Crayola crayon was born!

At first, Crayola's boxes held up to 30 colors. Over the next century, the company added more and more colors. Today's boxes hold up to 120 different shades! The boxes are sold in 80 countries around the world.

BOXES AND BOXES

Crayola creates more than 3 billion crayons each year!

PLANT AND BERRY WATERCOLOR PAINTS

CREATE WATERCOLORS USING THE PIGMENTS IN BERRIES AND SPINACH!

BERRY PAINTS

1 Pour 1 cup blackberries into a strainer sitting over a mixing bowl.

2 Use the spoon to smash the blackberries. Smash until you have squeezed out as much juice as possible.

3 Pour 1 tablespoon white vinegar into the juice. Add 1 teaspoon salt. These ingredients make the paint brighter and more colorful. Stir the mixture.

(continued on next page)

MATERIALS

blackberries
measuring cup
mesh strainer
mixing bowls
spoon

measuring spoons
white vinegar
salt
small storage containers
raspberries
spinach

sharp knife
cutting board
paintbrushes
paper

4 Pour the paint into a small container.

5 Repeat steps 1 through 4 with the raspberries.

SPINACH PAINT

1 Have an adult help you chop the spinach on the cutting board.

2 Place the strainer over a mixing bowl. Place the chopped spinach in the strainer.

3 Pour 1 tablespoon white vinegar over the spinach.

4 Use the measuring cup to press and grind the spinach. Squeeze out as much juice as possible.

5 Mix 1 teaspoon salt into the mixing bowl. Stir.

6 Pour the green juice into a small container.

PAINT!

1 Use your watercolors to paint on paper! Store the paints in the refrigerator for up to one week.

GLOW-IN-THE-DARK PAINT

BLEND POWDER AND GLUE TO MAKE PAINTINGS THAT GLOW!

MATERIALS

measuring cups
¼ cup glow-in-the-dark powder
¼ cup water
½ cup white all-purpose glue
mixing bowl
spoon
container
paintbrushes
paper

MEASURING AND MIXING

1 Add the glow-in-the-dark powder, water, and glue to the mixing bowl.

2 Stir the mixture with the spoon until well blended. Pour into a container.

3 Use the paint and paintbrushes to create a cool scene on the piece of paper.

4 Turn off the lights, and check out your glowing artwork!

TRY THIS!

Set your paint in the sun for 10 minutes. The sun will charge the paint, and it will glow even brighter in the dark!

WASHABLE WINDOW PAINT

WHIP UP THIS EASY PAINT, AND TURN A WINDOW INTO YOUR CANVAS!

1 Add ¼ cup dish soap and ½ cup tempera paint to a storage container. Stir.

2 Repeat step 1 using other paint colors.

3 Place an old towel under a window to catch drips. Then dip a foam brush or sponge in the paint. Now create some window art!

4 Use a damp towel to remove the paint when needed.

MATERIALS

dish soap
tempera paint
measuring cups

small storage containers
spoon
old towel
foam brush or sponge

COLORFUL CHALK CUBES

CREATE SUPERCOOL PIECES OF CHALK IN ICE CUBE TRAYS!

1. Measure and add ⅓ cup plaster of paris into the liquid measuring cup.

2. Add ¼ cup powdered paint. Stir.

3. Add ¼ cup water to the mixture. Stir.

4. Put the ice cube tray on a paper plate. Quickly pour the mix into the ice cube tray. Let the mix harden for 4 to 5 hours.

5. Repeat steps 1 through 4 to create more colors. Have fun using your chalk!

MATERIALS

measuring cups
plaster of paris
powdered paint

water
spoon
silicone ice cube
  tray
paper plate

TRINKET TREASURE CRAYONS

MAKE MULTICOLORED MELTED CRAYONS THAT HOLD SECRET TRINKETS!

FILLING THE MUFFIN PAN

1 Unwrap the paper from the crayon pieces. Break the crayons into several small pieces.

2 Fill each muffin cup halfway with crayon pieces. Group similar colors together in the cups.

3 Place one **trinket** in each muffin cup, resting on top of the crayons.

4 Fill each muffin cup with more broken crayons. Make sure they cover each trinket!

(continued on next page)

MATERIALS

old crayons
muffin pan
small trinkets
  (see list to
  the right)
oven mitts
cooling rack

SMALL TRINKETS MADE OF GLASS, STONE, OR METAL, SUCH AS:

coins
colorful stones
glass beads
glass gems
keys
marbles

BAKING AND COOLING

1 Have an adult help you heat the oven to 275 degrees Fahrenheit (135°C). Cook the crayons for about 10 minutes. If the crayons have not melted, cook them for another 10 minutes.

2 Use the oven mitt to remove the muffin pan. Then set the pan on the cooling rack for 10 minutes.

3 Place the muffin pan in the refrigerator for 20 minutes.

4 Remove the pan from the refrigerator, and gently shake the crayons out.

5 Give the crayons as gifts to friends and family. They will find the **trinkets** as they use them! Or, use the crayons yourself. Have fun finding out which trinket is inside each one.

GLOSSARY

advanced – a higher, more developed level.

canvas – a piece of cloth or material on which artists paint artwork.

colossal – huge, giant.

dissolve – to become part of a liquid.

medium – a substance used to create works of art.

pastime – an activity people do to pass time in a pleasant way.

pigment – a substance that gives something color.

saliva – watery fluid in the mouth.

trinket – a small object, such as a button, bead, toy, coin, or key.

WEBSITES

To learn more about Cool Toys & Games, visit **booklinks.abdopublishing.com**. These links are routinely monitored and updated to provide the most current information available.

INDEX